21st Century Junior Library

RECOGNIZIN
STRENGTHS AND ACTING

Emily Rose

Read and Reflect:
A Social-Emotional Guide

Published in the United States of America by:

Cherry Lake Press
2395 South Huron Parkway, Suite 200, Ann Arbor, Michigan 48104
www.cherrylakepress.com

Reading Adviser: Beth Walker Gambro, MS, Ed., Reading Consultant, Yorkville, IL
Photo Credits: © New Africa/Shutterstock.com, cover, 1; © Robert Kneschke/Shutterstock.com, 5; © wavebreakmedia/Shutterstock.com, 6; © Monkey Business Images/Shutterstock.com, 7; © Olha Tsiplyar/Shutterstock.com, 9; © APIWAN BORRIKONRATCHATA/Shutterstock.com, 10, 11; © Svetlana Krylatova/Shutterstock.com, 13 [top]; © kdshutterman/Shutterstock.com, 13 [bottom, right]; © thefisheystock/Shutterstock.com, 13 [bottom, left]; © Roman Samborskyi/Shutterstock.com, 14; © insta photos/Shutterstock.com, 16; © altanaska/Shutterstock.com, 19; © Lopolo/Shutterstock.com, 20 [right]; © vectorplus/Shutterstock.com, 20 [left]; © Prostock-studio/Shutterstock.com, 21

Cherry Lake Press is an imprint of Cherry Lake Publishing Group.

Library of Congress Cataloging-in-Publication Data

Names: Rose, Emily (School psychologist), author.
Title: Recognizing strengths and acting / by Emily Rose.
Description: Ann Arbor, Michigan : Cherry Lake Publishing, [2022] | Series: Read and reflect: a social-emotional guide | Includes bibliographical references and index. | Audience: Grades 2-3
Identifiers: LCCN 2021036755 (print) | LCCN 2021036756 (ebook) | ISBN 9781534199149 (hardcover) | ISBN 9781668900284 (paperback) | ISBN 9781668901724 (pdf) | ISBN 9781668906040 (ebook)
Subjects: LCSH: Ability in children—Juvenile literature. | Ability—Juvenile literature.
Classification: LCC BF723.A25 R58 2022 (print) | LCC BF723.A25 (ebook) | DDC 155.4/13—dc23
LC record available at https://lccn.loc.gov/2021036755
LC ebook record available at https://lccn.loc.gov/2021036756

Cherry Lake Press would like to acknowledge the work of the Partnership for 21st Century Learning, a Network of Battelle for Kids. Please visit http://www.battelleforkids.org/networks/p21 for more information.

Printed in the United States of America
Corporate Graphics

Cherry Lake Press

CONTENTS

What Is a Strength and Why People Need Different Strengths 4

How to Identify Your Strengths 10

How to Use Your Strengths 17

Extend Your Learning 20

Glossary 22

Find Out More 23

Index 24

About the Author 24

WHAT IS A STRENGTH AND WHY PEOPLE NEED DIFFERENT STRENGTHS

A strength is something that you are naturally good at. Sometimes we **compare** ourselves to others and wish we had the same strengths as they do. For example, you might really **admire** a famous basketball player and wish you could

What strengths do you admire in other people?

score three-pointers as easily as she can. It's normal to want what other people have, but the world needs people with lots of different strengths!

What is one strength you have that others might really wish they had?

What are some strengths that might be helpful for the world?

We need people who can shoot three-pointers, people who can make music, people who can listen to others and offer advice, and people who can practice medicine and take care of others.

Just imagine what the world would be like if everyone had the same strengths. It wouldn't work very well.

If everyone were a famous basketball player, we wouldn't have musicians, therapists, teachers, or doctors. That's why it is so great for people to have different strengths. Then we have lots of different professionals who can make the world a better place!

Make a Guess!

Describe a world in which everyone has the same strengths. What does that world look like?

Is there something that people often ask you for help with?

HOW TO IDENTIFY YOUR STRENGTHS

It can be easy to see strengths in other people but much harder to see strengths in ourselves. That's because a strength is usually something that comes easily to us, so we might not even realize it's a strength!

One way to **identify** your strengths is to think of the things that people ask you to do for them. Do your friends always ask for your

help with their math homework or to help them fix their video game when the screen freezes? You might have a strength in math or in understanding **technology** that you didn't even think of before!

To discover your strengths, try thinking of what is easy for you or what you like to do. We usually like to do things that are easy for us, and things that are easy for us are often strengths! Another way you can identify your strengths is to ask other people what they think your strengths are. Easy, right? Sometimes other people can offer another **perspective** that helps us see things that we might not notice on our own.

What things come easily to you that other people might find difficult?

Ask a friend or parent what they think your strengths are. Do you agree or disagree?

For example, your teacher might tell you that your writing is very good. After hearing this, you might remember that you usually get good grades on writing assignments and writing feels easy to you. This could mean that you have a strength in writing.

Think!

Think of one of your friends. What do you think that person's strengths are? Write them down and tell them next time you see them. You might just help them learn something new about themselves!

Now that you have an idea what your strengths might be, list ways you can use them!

HOW TO USE YOUR STRENGTHS

Once you have a clearer idea of what your strengths are, think about how to use them. If you can fix your friends' frozen video game screens, you might want to use your knowledge of **electronics** by joining a **robotics** or computer club.

If you find it easy to write essays in English class, maybe you could join a local young authors' group or write letters to nursing homes or hospitals in your community. That way, you can both use and improve your writing skills!

You never know how useful your strengths might turn out to be in the future or how you could use them to help someone else. Maybe your strengths in electronics

Ask Questions!

Write down one or two ways you can use or develop your current strengths. Ask a teacher or adult for help.

will lead you to become a video game designer, computer engineer, or electrician one day! Or you might use your writing skills to be a children's book author, poet, journalist, or speechwriter.

Take some time to think about what your strengths might be. Imagine what you might be able to do with them one day to make the world a better place!

Think of a strength that you have. How might you use that strength in your future career?

EXTEND YOUR LEARNING

Sometimes it can be hard for us to see our own strengths. That is why it can help to ask your friends and family to help you identify your strengths. It's also normal to feel **jealous** of other people's strengths or want to have those strengths too.

When you feel jealous of someone else's strengths, think of ways that you can remind yourself that the world needs different strengths, and your strengths are **valuable** too! Some examples might be to use positive

self-talk, or say some nice things about yourself, and think of all the things you do well.

Now that you have thought about your strengths, list some ways that you can use your strengths to help you grow in different places. For example, if you are really good at drawing, how might this help you with class assignments or art projects? If you are really good at waiting your turn in line, how might this **patience** help you when you play a sport?

Remember, everyone has different strengths, and that is a great thing!

GLOSSARY

admire (uhd-MYRE) regard with wonder or respect

compare (kuhm-PAYR) to note similarities or differences between people or things

develop (dih-VEH-luhp) to make better or improve

electronics (ih-lek-TRAH-niks) devices that use electricity to operate

identify (eye-DEN-tuh-fye) to recognize or notice

jealous (JEH-luhs) wanting what someone else has

patience (PAY-shuhns) the ability to wait for something without getting upset

perspective (puhr-SPEK-tiv) viewpoint

robotics (roh-BAH-tiks) the field that uses computer-operated devices that can do tasks

technology (tek-NAH-luh-jee) use of science or engineering to improve products or processes

valuable (VAL-yuh-buhl) having value, important

FIND OUT MORE

Books

Byers, Grace. *I Am Enough.* New York, NY: HarperCollins, 2018.

DiTerlizzi, Angela. *The Magical Yet.* Los Angeles, CA: Disney-Hyperion, 2020.

Websites

Power of the Pen

https://powerofthepen.org
Find a local writers' group like Power of the Pen to develop your strength in writing.

YouTube—Identifying Your Strengths

https://www.youtube.com/watch?v=JwNI1F21eK8
Watch this video and learn the importance of finding your strengths.

INDEX

comparisons, 4, 6

easy things, 10, 12, 15

jealousy, 20

perspective, 12

self-talk, positive, 20–21
strengths
  extending your learning about, 20–21
  identifying, 10–15, 20–21
  importance of different, 4–9, 20
  using, 16–19, 21
  what they are, 4–9

ABOUT THE AUTHOR

Emily Rose is a school psychologist, yoga teacher, and writer for her mental wellness blog, MissMagnoliaSays.com. She enjoys helping kids and adults understand and manage their emotions and live beautiful lives. Emily lives in Dearborn, Michigan.